To the small brown birds.

Published by Curly Press
Boho South, Victoria, Australia

First published by Curly Press, 2024

Design by Lavinia Hartney © Lavinia Hartney Designs
Cover artwork by Michael Leunig
Collected and compiled by Nicola Dierich

Printed and bound in Australia by
McPherson's Printing Group, Maryborough, Victoria

ISBN 978 0 646 70073 1

leunig.com.au

NEWSPAPER
POEMS

Also by Michael Leunig

NEWSPAPER POEMS

MICHAEL LEUNIG

Poetry & Drawings

Contents

Introduction

The poems and verses in this collection, with a couple of exceptions, were written as part of my newspaper cartooning work over the past sixty years. It always seemed to me that a newspaper cartoon could be more than a cutting witticism or clever joke with a neat punchline. What I loved most was a fey mysterious element in cartoons; the feral, elusive particle that could haunt or outflank the rational political intellect.

A long time ago, I presented one of my more peculiar cartoons to an editor right on deadline. He stared at it and scratched his head. "I don't understand this," he said in a baffled voice, as he looked me in the eye. There was a long silence as he stared quizzically at my drawing, and then came his memorable words: "But... I like it!" he said, with a startled shake of his head and an impish smile of acceptance. My heart lifted, the cartoon was published, a huge lesson was learned and a great blessing bestowed. "I don't understand it but I like it". Such wonderful liberating words to remember ⸴ for the artist and for the soul.

Beginning with a wealth of nursery rhymes, schoolyard clapping songs and slang verses, I grew up surrounded by short poems, many of them wonderfully mysterious, absurd, unsavoury or simply terrific fun to chant in the street with friends. And there were my mother's magazine clippings of small verses stuck to the cupboard door in the kitchen.

All of this was folk poetry; much of it learned from parents, grandmothers and the local working class vernacular. Its rhymes and rhythms, brevity, emotion and naughtiness held it together and ensured its survival.

It's in the lingering spirit of this old form that the pieces in this book were written, mostly as I made my way to a cartoon deadline for a newspaper. At such times, words and images can be such good friends.

As part of this inherited feeling, I included an underlying cheekiness, which in this situation is the unusual appearance of a heartfelt, lyrical sentiment in a newspaper cartoon; indeed a departure from the tradition of social commentary cartooning in a serious daily newspaper. Such an offering may seem naive or irrelevant to the sociologist, the political scientist, or the academic prude, but all the more reason to do it, said the long-suffering creative daredevil in me! Please forgive the 'preachy' bits in this collection; a tiny sermon wrapped in some doggerel is a useful domestic tradition.

These verses, originally illustrated rather obliquely with cartoonish handmade drawings, often made a happy and mysterious synthesis for me; they seemed to be more than the sum of their parts. It may be a small thing but this was the mysterious creative risk that lured me onwards to the rejection of smart punchlines and towards the chance of inventive discovery that was simple, light, peculiar and possibly profound.

These public verses were mostly heartfelt and in earnest - which is not the normal bedfellow of satirical drawings or dire editorial pronouncements. So why would an incurable jester offer to the world a verse which revealed parts of the vulnerable serious self? Wasn't this a corny lapse into self indulgence? Wasn't this betraying the old game of cool professional nonchalance? Perhaps so, but that may have been the price of innocent experimental pleasure and the joyous impulse.

Having said that, I must also say that in spite of all I write here, I still chuckle with delight to hear a clever joke or a brilliant witticism, even though my own newspaper creations have been more playful and whimsical. You see, I believe that a whim can be a greatly underrated impulse and a valuable gift from the unconscious - and playfulness can be an inspired way forward when the world becomes too clever and cold. I have always been tempted by the idea of being serious when everybody is laughing and making humour when the world has grown too sombre and grim.

The drawings in this collection did not accompany the original verses. They are more recent doodles made just for fun. It is a sweet, spiritual delight to make a small drawing that has never previously existed anywhere in the world.

A Fly In The Ointment

In every darkness is a healing joy
In every happiness a disappointment
And in the hopes of every girl and boy
A fly is often in the ointment.

A little fly; a humble tiny life
A wayward, unexpected winged thing
Has introduced all purity to strife
And made the angels weep and laugh and sing.

A Great Big Autumn Leaf

If I get old
I'll turn to gold
And orange, brown or red;
The wind will blow
And I'll let go
And float out of my bed;
I'll flutter up across the sky
Beyond this world of grief;
Away up high I'm going to fly:
A great big Autumn leaf.

A Little Duck

With a bit of luck
A duck
Will come into your life
When you are at the peak
Of your great powers
And your achievement towers
like a smoking chimney stack
There'll be a quack
And right there at your feet
A little duck will stand;
She will take you by the hand
And lead you
Like a child with no defence;
She will lead you
Into wisdom, joy and innocence.
That little duck.
We wish you luck.

A Moment

Life is a donkey. What a surprise!
The trees in the park are graceful and wise.
Love is sanity. Sanity is love.
So sings the blackbird, so said the dove.

Such is the moment. Here is the rain.
Death is a flower. Gone is the pain.
Nothing beneath you, nothing above.
Love is sanity. Sanity is love.

A Winter's Poem

A clever creature is the snake,
Who spends his winters not awake;
He snuggles in his long thin bed
And brews up venom in his head.

The human is a different sort;
He spends the winter watching sport;
He yells abuse in concrete stands
And empties out his poison glands.

Absence

Absence makes the heart grow fonder.

Distance makes the feelings wander.

Patience calms the day completely.

Silence makes the bird sing sweetly.

Ah, This...

Between the head, the heart and the little toe
There is mystery and genius
There is war and woe
There is love and madness
There is right and wrong
There's a painting, a friend and a beautiful song

And above this toe and this heartfelt head
There is more, much more than could ever be said.
Beasts and angels and all things odd
You can hold it all and call it God.

Artist, Leave The World of Art

Artist, leave the world of art,
Pack your goodies on a cart,
Duck out through some tiny hole,
Slip away and save your soul.

Leave no footprints, don't look back,
Take the dark and dirty track.
Cross the border, cross your heart:
Freedom from the world of art.

At The Top

At the top of the
tallest building in
the world...

... sat the saddest
man in the world;

and inside the man was
the loneliest heart in
the world

and inside the heart
was the deepest pit
in the world

and at the bottom of
the pit was the
blackest mud in the world

and in the mud lay
the lightest, loveliest, tenderest,
most beautiful happy angel
in the universe.
So things weren't so bad after all.

Autumn

Leaves are falling and revealing
One of winter's eerie sights:
On the trees, how unappealing,
Wire for the fairy lights.

Wire with plastic insulation
Stapled onto every limb;
Circuits in the vegetation
Indicate that life is grim.

Misery in any city
Can be measured, if you please,
By counting with the eye of pity
Fairy lights installed in trees.

Autumn Leaves

In every heart where Autumn leaves are falling,
In every man an angel and an ape,
In every loving soul an ancient calling,
The genius for freedom and escape.

In every leaf the beauty of its dying,
The memory of coloured summer days.
In men of worldly power their glorifying
The dullness of their failing, worn out ways.

Autumn Prayer

Oh easy-going, lovely natured thing
Come gently to this troubled life and bring
Good humour, sweet forgiveness, love and grace,
Bring gratitude and peace upon this place.
Feed our sorrows to the morning birds,
May their songs bring truth into our words,
In sadness let us feel each other's worth,
Turn our lonely losses into earth.

Beer Glass

Descended from the working class
He stared into his beer glass
A Celtic, Anglo-Saxon chap
Not much fell into his lap.

No dreaming tales, no promised land
No history to understand.
And yet he had his dialect
Funny, raw and incorrect.

It helped him find his way through life
And find his chirpy second wife
A steady soul, an uncut gem
No hate speech could diminish them.

He knew that everything would pass
And stared into his beer glass.

Boyhood Poem

I was alone a lot.
I lived a life that I forgot.
I was broken.
I was mended.
I pretended I was loved.
Bits of me were shoved
Against a wall;
The wall I tried to climb
So I could spend some time
With love and joy and you;
The things that every boy
Believes are true.
What is God?
Who am I?
Why is the sky so blue?
Why is the night so black?
Why and who and what?
I was alone a lot.

Brain Plasticity

Brain plasticity: what is that?!
My lovely brain is going flat!
Like a battery that's exhausted.
No lively spark. What has caused it?
This fading of lucidity?
Is it mass stupidity
And the grinding ugliness,
The silly, noisy, man-made mess
To which we find ourselves exposed?
The pathways of the brain get closed.
The mind begins to warp and shrink.
It's getting very hard to think
With so much nonsense going on.
Where's the joyful thinking gone?
The lovely eccentricity?
Help me brain plasticity!

Care Is The Cure

Care is the cure.
It is slow,
It is raw,
It is pure.

It is simple and bare.
It is real,
It is bold,
It is there.

Nothing is newer
Or older,
Or wiser,
Or truer.
Care is the cure.

Carol

The three wise birds are on their way
To Bethlehem to sing and pray
And welcome in the holy day
When peace on earth will come to stay

And they will try and try again
To sing some love back into men;
This old and weary mother hen
This blackbird and a tiny wren.

Cheerful

It's love that makes the world go round
But fear can do it faster
You quickly cover lots of ground
When heartache is the master.

Of course it may not feel like fear
Or dread or desperation,
It feels like something near and dear:
Excitement and elation!

But fear it is that makes you bleed
And speeding makes you fearful
Nothing can be loved at speed
Love is slow and cheerful.

Coercive Control

Coercive control:
It isn't much fun
But isn't this how
the country is run?
The carrot, the stick,
the jail, the fine;
Isn't this how
we're all kept in line?
And yet you are warned
that coercive control
Is a terrible crime
to the heart and the soul.

So do as they say
and not as they do
Or something coercive
will happen to you.

Consent

"May I sit quietly with you?"
"Yes, you may."

"Can I talk of life and death with you?"
"Yes, you can."

"Can I have some time to know you more and be
myself with you?"
"Yes, you can."

"May I cook a meal with you and can we eat it together?"
"Yes, we can."

"Can I make mistakes with you and be forgiven?"
"Yes, you can. Yes, yes, yes."

"And... Can I make a garden with you?"
"Yes of course. Let's do it."

Daffodil

When the storm has passed,
As it will,
You may see a daffodil.

When four mad winds
Have torn the trees apart
When cold and fearful was
the human heart,
When poison words have burned
and looks could kill,
You may see a daffodil.

And when the wheel has turned.
When all your precious days are done
And you become the earth
That loves the rain and sun,
As you will.
You may be a daffodil.

Dear Soul

Mother dear mother, what is my duty?
Truth and love, compassion and beauty.
Father dear father, what is my song?
Soulful, mysterious, tender and strong.
Sister dear sister, how do we know?
Joyful and humble, painful and slow.
Brother dear brother, why do we live?
To see, to feel, to grieve and forgive.
God my dear God, what do you say?
The flower, the bee, the music, the day
Dear heart of mine, what can I do?
Make peace and make way for all that is true.

Dog

The news was bad
The day was cold
The world grew sad
As I grew old.
Then as I neared
Catastrophe
A dog appeared
And smiled at me.
It smiled at me
It smiled at ME
A dog came up
And smiled at me!

Don't Give Up

Don't give up. Go to the kitchen.
Make a cup of something warm.
Outside, the storm is cold and mad.
The soul is strong and old and sad.

Don't lose heart. Go to the kitchen.
There is an art in holding on
To what is fair and true and good
You learned it here in childhood.

Don't let go. Be in the kitchen.
Be clear and slow. Forgive your fear.
The goodness here will nourish you
Enjoy your love for what is true.

Don't give up.

Driverless Car

I went last night in a driverless car
To a soulless place with a charmless bar
For a tasteless meal with a joyless date;
What a pointless, mindless, useless state.
She said, "What a lifeless thing you are!"
So home I went in my driverless car.

Duck Study

How you will know
If a person,
Perhaps a politician, a policeman,
A partner or a priest,
Is corrupt:
You must study the duck.
You must play with the duck.
You must talk with the duck.
You must know the ways of the duck.
You must look deeply into the eyes of the duck.
Then, looking into the face of the person,
How will you know if that person is corrupt?
You will know.
YOU WILL KNOW.

Duet (song and dance for Mr. Curly and Vasco Pyjama)

You understand the many things
That I don't understand.
And I can understand the things
That you don't understand.
Both of us stand under things
That we had never planned.
How it came to be like this
We both don't understand.

This is how we find each other.
This is how we care.
This is how we love each other
This is what we share.

Epiphany

Amid the great cacophony
Of angry words and commentary,
A sudden bright epiphany.

It was small and soft and clear,
It was far and it was near,
A little bird was in my ear.

And all the endless arguments
The fierce aggression and defence
Quite suddenly made little sense.

Instead the secret of the bird,
So vast and deep and true was heard.
It only sang one simple word.

F Word

We can't say the F word
Or else we will be smitten
We don't say the N word
Or else we could be bitten
We won't say the S word
For then we might be lashed
We can't say the P word
For fear of being bashed
But we can say the C word
And no one will be surly
We can say it loud and clear:
Curly, curly, curly!

For Now

Get well
Do good
Make love
Touch wood
Be kind
Be true
Get well
Be you.

Genius

The long forgotten genius within;
The tender innocence beneath the skin,
Living like a pixie in the wild:
The soulful genius of every child
That calls the heart to be alone and rare
And rapturous and rather strange, and dare
To sing the songs of joy into the land
And say the prayers that none can understand
To ancestors, the blazing stars at night
Who gave you all this mystery and delight.

Get A Life

Anyone can get a life.
Anyone can lose it
But who will dare to inhabit the thing
And use it?

A lived in life will soon get loose and worn
from use and feeling;
Countless tiny scratches;
The shine goes off.
It's very unappealing!

Dirt builds up,
A load of muck and grit.
A part of you gets lost–
A hope, a philosophy
Or a love that doesn't fit.

Another broken sleep.
A dream collapses.
A quick repair. It's worth a try.
A scrap of string for the soul.
Perhaps a battered grin will fill the hole–
Or just a sigh.

Flakes and cracks!
A major idea buckles badly
A makeshift support is invoked quickly.
A tired old joke could hide the dint.
Or be a wedge, or a patch, or a splint...
Truly, sweetly, sadly.

And yet it works and lives!
It all still goes. It forgives.
It's a miracle!
Worn in, bashed in, cried in,
And the great thing–
A lived in life
Can be happily died in.

Give

Give your heart to the outer reaches
Give your mind to the birds
Give your love to peculiar creatures
Give some soul to your words
Give some cheer to the sad old geezers
Give some thanks for the odd.
Give unto Caesar what is Caesar's
But give your art to God.

God Give Me A Quite Week

God give me a quiet week,
Nothing too amazing,
Nothing too far up the creek,
I need to do some grazing.

God please let me simply plod
A path that's not too rough.
Being me is very odd
And that is quite enough.

God Give Us Rain

God give us rain when we expect sun.
Give us music when we expect trouble.
Give us tears when we expect breakfast.
Give us dreams when we expect a storm.
Give us a stray dog when we expect congratulations.
God play with us, turn us sideways and around.

Amen.

Going to Sleep

Now I lay me down to sleep
With fragments drifting from the deep;
The mysteries, the love and strife,
The wild creature that is life;
This life I do not understand,
The grieving heart, the open hand,
A careful step, a joyful leap,
The dream before we go to sleep,
The crazy world, a simple breath,
The life before we go to death,
The silver moon, the little town,
As in the dark I lay me down.

Good Old Love

Oh my God, it's five to seven
Time to get up and go to heaven;
Heaven on earth, a smile, a frown,
Don't let the mastheads grind you down.

Life's too beautiful for some
Who thinks that life should be more glum
And overruled and more controlled
But love of life is brave and bold.

Life's a miracle, life is wise
Joy is life's great sweet surprise.
Love a duck and pat a hound
And spread this good old love around.

Gratitude And Grief

In the cradle of his mother's arms a baby lies
Warm and sheltered from the time when they will come apart
Gazing from the hidden world into his mother's eyes
From where the holy secrets tumble down into his heart.

Then with this heart so full of hope he travels in the wild
But soon is set upon and cruelly beaten to the ground
And wakes upon the ruins of his innocence defiled
And there his sacred revelations in the mud are found.

Tears of blood and anger flowing from his wounded eye
From his violated mouth the song of disbelief
In his shattered memory a shattered lullaby
But from his broken heart flow gratitude and grief.

He Lost His Mind

He lost his mind. It happened gently. It felt natural.

It wandered off on a quiet Saturday afternoon.

By the time darkness fell it had not returned.

He enjoyed his dinner. He listened to music. He felt relieved.

A beautiful sense of simplicity entered into him.

Before bed he went outside and smiled at the stars.

Somewhere faraway in the world his mind wandered like a happy old dog, like an autumn leaf, like a carefree child.

Hesitancy

In the aged care facility we call the earth
Hesitancy starts soon after birth;
Hesitant to do what we need to do,
Hesitant to accept what may be true,
Hesitant to be as we really are,
Twinkle, twinkle little star,
To step out brightly and go forth
Toward true life, true love, true north.

True goodness never comes too late
And kindness does not hesitate.

High-Vis

There he is
The man in high-vis
Holding a sign
They're painting a line
On the road ahead.
His helmet is red
The sign says 'SLOW'
I say hello.
He says g'day
He turns away
He gives a cough
I drive off
Our friendship small
I loved it all
This way of his
The man in high-vis.

How To Get There

Go to the end of the path until you get to the gate.

Go through the gate and head straight out towards
the horizon.

Keep going towards the horizon.

Sit down and have a rest every now and again,

But keep on going, just keep on with it.

Keep on going as far as you can.

That's how you get there.

Hymn

Little flower let us pray
The world gets madder every day
There's little I can understand
The anxious hearts, the broken land.

All I want to know is you
Your leaves so green, your petals blue
Your beautiful humility
Are made of love and sanity.

Little flower let us pray
Together in this childish way
For there within your petals curled
Lies wisdom that would heal the world.

In Every Beast

In every beast there is a man,
In every man there is a boy,
In every boy there is a girl,
In every girl a wild pearl
That grows into a wild tree.

In every tree there is a bird,
In every bird there is a song,
In every song is joy and grief,
In love and life a lovely beast.
In every beast there is a man.

In One Ear

In one ear and out the other,
Words of wisdom, milk of mother,
Songs of birds, the joyful years,
Loneliness and love and tears.

Pain and failure, sweet relief,
Brutal honesty and grief
Come and go and disappear,
Our heart becomes the last frontier.

And so you enter like a child,
Your innocence is pure and wild.
Oh dear sister, oh dear brother,
Love this life then live the other.

In Winter

In winter we grow old.
Nothing else will grow.
Except the mould upon our thinking.
The world feels lost and sad and low.
Sanity and love are sinking.

And yet, there in the cold and rainy street
A little smile as warm as toast
Appears upon a passing stranger's face
For one sweet second there is grace
When eye meets eye we see the holy ghost.

Then onwards through the dying light we go.
Through a rushing world of deep unknowing
Reminded of the beauty that we know.
Winter is a time for knowing.

Into Weariness And Woe

Into weariness and woe
I am bound to simply go,
Understanding less and less
Of this existential mess.
Not to stagger or to stoop
But to bear this bowl of soup
With careful steadiness and cheer;
This soup I made, this bowl so dear,
This time on earth, these bits I found,
The trembling heart, the shaky ground,
The fading light, the wistful moon,
My winding path, my wooden spoon.

It Is

It is, it is,
sang the wonderful bird.
It is what it is
Is the song that I heard.

It is, it is,
said the duck and the fish,
Your life and the world
are not what you wish.

But simply it is,
it's the teapot, the moon,
The song of the bird
and its beautiful tune.

It Is Finished

It is finished.
So let us share
These dear remaining moments;
A tiny scoop of air,
Two more little touches of your hand
The final touches,
And we'll be there.

It is done
And love is here
Not as it was before;
Beneath a world of fear;
For now the world is just a tiny flower,
The light is true
And love is near.

It is gone:
The living pain;
The steady ache for power,
The agony for gain;
Like a fever which has faded now,
And only light
And love remain.

For love was made
In spite of all,
Piece by lonely piece;
Fragments frail and small
And dearly held when life was cold, was dark;
Now love's the light
That holds it all.
It is there
And it is true;
The final touches now
Will see it gently through;
Two more little touches of your hand
Love for me
And love for you.

It Is Spring

It is Spring.
The world is mad.
The children sing.
The birds are glad.
The flowers grow.
The bees are keen.
The rivers flow.
The air is clean.
The lass will meet
The joyful lad.
The sun is sweet
The world is mad.

JOMO *(Joy Of Missing Out)*

Oh the joy of missing out.
When the world begins to shout
And rush towards that shining thing;
The latest bit of mental bling –
Trying to have it, see it, do it,
You simply know you won't go through it;
The anxious clamouring and need
This restless hungry thing to feed.
Instead, you feel the loveliness;
The pleasure of your emptiness.
You spurn the treasure on the shelf
In favour of your peaceful self;
Without regret, without a doubt.
Oh the joy of missing out.

La-La Land

I want to go to La-La Land
And have a holiday;
In La-La Land they'll understand
The thing I have to say.

I'll rent the little wonky shack
That overlooks the bay
And wait until it all comes back,
This thing I have to say.

And then one night I'll bow my head
While strolling on the sand
And say the thing that must be said
Out loud in La-La Land.

Lesson

There's a sausage on the table
And a dog upon the floor
The cook steps out to take a break
And shuts the kitchen door,
But soon the break is over
The cook has now returned
To a non-existent sausage
And a lesson to be learned.

Let It Go

Let it go. Let it out.
Let it all unravel.
Let it free and it can be
A path on which to travel.

Life Is Cruel Enough

Life is cruel enough
And horribly unjust
Then why must humans be so tough
And ruthless... and so cruel
And truthless?

Remember now my crazy friend
Everybody gets it in the end
It's wiser sometimes to be tender
The only victory is the peace
Of deep surrender.

Painful weakness comes to all
For just as children die
As bombs do fall and cities burn
In one way or another
Every man and every mother
Everybody gets their lonely turn.

But now the year is growing tired
As it struggles to the mournful end
Make something that will be of worth
And never end
Make beauty on this weary earth
Make love dear sad humanity
My lonely broken friend.

Little Fish

The little fish that wants to swim in me
The fish of joy that leaps into the sun
The fish of love, the fish of mystery
Oh little fish forgive what I have done

The wild stream that wants to flow in me
The stream of hope that sparkles in the sun
The stream of grief, the stream of memory
Oh wild stream forgive what I have done

Human nature is a wild place
Terrible and beautiful to know
Wilderness of violence and grace
Valleys where the soul is found to grow
To this land I travelled in a dream
There I made my secret, lonely wish
There I wept into the wild stream
And I kneel before you now my little fish

The little bird that wants to sing in me
The song we hear when all is said and done
Fly my little bird for you are free
Lift your heart and sing for everyone.

Little Rock

Do not mock the little rock,
After you are dead and gone
The rock remains to carry on;
Steady, true and still;
Sitting in the sunshine on the hill.

Little Tendrils

Little tendrils of the heart,
Curling out and groping,
Seeking little things to hold,
Wiggling and hoping.
Little tendrils of the soul,
Delicate and perky,
Seeking little surfaces,
Peculiar and quirky.
Little tendrils, little tendrils,
Innocent and plucky,
I pray that you are careful
And I hope that you are lucky.

Love And Fear

There are only two feelings
Love and fear.
There are only two languages
Love and fear.
There are only two activities
Love and fear.
There are only two motives,
two procedures, two frameworks,
two results;
Love and fear. Love and fear.

Love Goes On

Nature is beautiful, brutal and wise
The birds work hard, they don't tell lies
They have a voice, it's the voice of God
It says that you are wonderfully odd
It says your heart has a broken wing
That our soul has pain and truth can sting
That clouds have rain and bells will ring
That love goes on and God will sing.

Love Is Born

Love is born
With a dark and troubled face,
When hope is dead
And in the most unlikely place;
Love is born,
Love is always born.

Love One Another

Love one another and you will be happy.
It's as simple and difficult as that.
There is no other way.

Love Song *(For Strange Times)*

Life is suffering, love is good.
Love and care are made of wood.
Trees are made of soil and stars.
The wisdom of a thousand scars
Will make it gently understood
That life is suffering, love is good.

Magpie

Magpie, magpie, dive on me,
Swoop down from your holy tree;
As I pass the flower bed
Stick your beak into my head.

Magpie, magpie, make a hole,
Through my head into my soul;
As I pass beneath the sun
Bring my troubled head undone.

Magpie, magpie, it is spring,
Is my soul a happy thing?
As I pass around the tree
Make a hole so you can see.

Mid-Winter Blues

The mid-winter blues
begins in your shoes
Then crawls up your legs
to your knickers
Your heart goes all glum
as the life in your bum
Gets weaker and
everything flickers.

Yet a wee nip of Scotch
and a rain storm to watch
Are pleasures that
carry you through;
Or the gurgling gutter,
some fresh bread and butter
With a warm plate of
old-fashioned stew.

Mr. Curly's Summer Confession

Oh the pain and grief, the guilt and shame
For all the times in life when I was lame
With them, with him, with her, with me and you:
My sorrow for the things I did not do.

The holy duck I did not think to follow,
The joyous offerings I would not swallow,
The trees I never spoke to in the dawn,
The death of creatures I had failed to mourn.

The loss of innocence, the loss of heart,
The loveliness in which I took no part,
The happiness from which I turned away
And all the prayers of love I did not pray.

Muddle Through

I do my best to muddle through,
It's really all that we can do;
Through the mess, through the stress,
Understanding less and less,
Nothing certain, nothing sure,
Yet I feel I'm feeling more.
And it feels so right and good
Going back to childhood.

My Big Toe

My big toe is an honest man
So down to earth and normal;
Always true unto himself
And pleasantly informal;
Full of simple energy,
Contented with his role
If all of me was more like him
I'd be a happy soul.

No Sooner

No sooner do you arrive than it's time to leave.

How beautiful it is. How glorious. Yet it's nearly time to go...
So you take it in,
You take it in...

... and you gather a few small souvenirs: some leaves...
lavender, rosemary, eucalyptus.
A few small pebbles
A few small secrets
A look you received
Nine little notes of music...
and then... it's time to go.

You move towards the open door and
the silent night beyond...
the few bright stars...
a deep breath...
and it really is time to go.

No sooner does it all begin to make sense;
does it start to come true; does it all open up;
do you begin to see;
does it enter into your heart...

... No sooner do you arrive than it's time to leave.
Yes, it's the truth... and...
... and then you will have passed through it—
and with mysterious consequence it will have passed
through you.

Non-Consensual

I blew a non-consensual kiss
Into the night of peaceful air
An act of gratitude and bliss
It came to earth quite everywhere.

I was in love with life at last
I was in love with mother earth
In spite of all the painful past
I felt the miracle of birth.

And so the kiss comes back to me
Returns to us, comes back to you
So beautiful, so strong and free
So everywhere, so real and true.

Nowhere

The more that you travel
The less you recall
The closer you get
To nowhere at all.
The statue of David
The streets of New York
The pull of the journey
The plates of pulled pork.
You eat all the dishes
You drink all the wines
You follow the masses
You follow the signs.
You see all the places
You do all the things
You have a wild moment
While spreading your wings.
Priority boarding
They're giving the call
As closer you get
To nowhere at all.

Nude

From the dream inside our mother's womb,
We come into the crowded noisy room
Of life on earth.

Our birth is rude.
We come completely nude.
The soul is raw.
Our skin is bare.
At first we feel the air
And there and then the naked breast is found.
All of life is soft and warm and round,

The nipple and the lips so pink and ripe and new,
The newborn mouth knows what to do,
And skin is pressed excitedly to skin
As memories of feel and touch begin
In loves' first blissful primal kiss.
And every kiss forevermore will be a bit like this.

For skin holds memories of touch,
The sight or feel of nakedness awakens much.
And skin begins to feel a need for skin
The stirrings of the memory within.

The milk and rapture of the mother's breast
The love of skin to skin will never rest;
By grace and innocence compelled:
The need to hold, and to be held.

Just to hold a hand or stroke a brow.
The tingling of the naked touch returns the soul
unconsciously somehow
To warmth and nudity with mother at the start,
When we were happiest in our naked little heart
Than we would be for evermore.
And so we touch ourselves,
Or touch each other and explore
The beauty and the miracle of skin;
The sensuous memory unbeknown within.

To kiss grandmother's cheek,
To feel a lover's hand upon your arm
The hand that rubs our back until we're calm.
To taste the new-found lips, the strange caress.
To yearn for total nakedness.
Of self and other.
A bright reincarnation of a sacred time with mother.
Far beyond the realms of love or joy or sin.
Oh the wonder and the longing in our naked skin.

Obstacle Course

Life is an obstacle course, of course
The world goes mad, a sad divorce
From old beliefs you thought would hold
A light turns red, some friends turn cold.

Things don't work like they used to work
Another army goes beserk
You lose your faith in human kind
You lose your keys, you lose your mind.

With lonely heart and troubled head
You find your way to a garden bed
And there a beautiful flower has grown
Through obstacles and threats unknown
A peaceful powerful gentle force
Life is an obstacle course, of course.

Ode To A Jet-Ski Person

Jet-ski person, selfish fink,
May your silly jet-ski sink.
May you hit a pile of rocks,
Oh hoonish, summer coastal pox.

Noisy smoking dickhead fool,
On your loathsome leisure tool,
Give us all a jolly lark
And sink beside a hungry shark.

Scream as in its fangs you go:
Your last attention-seeking show,
While on the beach we all join in,
With, "three cheers for the dorsal fin!"

Off The Grid

The best thing they did
Was to get off the grid
The grid that sends out the lies

The gross propaganda
The fear and the slander
That keeps everyone down to size.

The dirty old tricks
The bad politics
Celebrities, fashions and fame

The stupid ideas
The despicable cheers
A delusional world going lame

So they got off the grid
And off came the lid
And out came a world that was true

And they laughed 'til they cried
And they lived 'til they died
Having done the best thing
They could do.

Olive Tree

Lovely dreaming olive tree
Oh the way you look at me
With your multitude of eyes,
Dark and shiny, strong and wise.
Let me drift into your gaze
Dreaming of the summer days
Of love and light and you and me,
Oh lovely dreaming olive tree.

On A Hill

A man sat quietly on a hill
The moon sat on his head
A friend sat smiling in his heart
The smiling friend was dead.

They spoke together in the dark
Beneath the milky way
They said the words from years ago
That they had failed to say.

A meteor fell gently down
The wise old moon had shone
The stars then sang their words of love
And life continued on.

Once In A Lifetime

Once in a lifetime a beautiful light
Will sparkle from the deepest black
And help you through the lonely night.
Once you go there's no way back.

Do not seek the lovely glow,
Hear carefully, speak prayerfully
with everyone,
It happened for you long ago,
It is good and it is done.

Our Father

Our father – can't be found
He worked himself into the ground.
He did his best, he did it tough
And yet it wasn't good enough.

Our father, who was he?
He threw himself into the sea;
The sea of love so deep and wild
Man enough to be a child.

Our father, who are you?
Will you live to see it through?
It's been sad and it's been rough.
Father it's been good enough.

Pat The Dog

Pat the dog, pat the cat
Pat each other just like that.
When you fail, when I fall
We don't have to speak at all
Just reach out and touch this hand.
Who could ever understand?
Touch my arm, stroke my head
There is little to be said.
Pat the dog, pat the cat
Pat me softly just like that.

Peace Is My Drug

Peace is my drug;
It stops the pain.
In safe reflecting rooms
Or in a lane,
Or in a park,
I will lie
And have some peace
And get high.
If it's pure
And there's a lot of it about
I overdose
And pass out
And dream of peace:
My favourite thing
When nobody wants me
And nothing's happening.

Permission To Evaporate

Unexpectedly it disappeared one night ⸰
This need of mine;
This need to be,
This need to make it right,
The necessity to see,
To know, to care, to find and understand,
To feel, to give, to make, to doubt,
To laugh or weep,
To keep on being me ⸰
The whole thing just wore out
And I was free.
It came to be, it fell out of the blue ⸰
Permission to evaporate came through.

I suddenly became thin air,
Or even less;
Neither here nor there,
But everywhere I guess,
And nowhere too.
I turned to spirit;
The perfect shooting through.
Beyond all space and time
A lifetime's wear and tear

Was made sublime.
A quick and airy little gasp was done
As up I went into the moon and sun,
Like some fading floating song.
It made such perfect sense:
No stain, no trace, no evidence.
No need to leave or to belong.
No need to think or calculate;
I simply just accepted it for free.
What life had given me -
Permission to evaporate.

Pitiful And Beautiful
(Oh Tiny Little Thing)

Pitiful and beautiful oh tiny little thing
I got down on my knee to see a tiny little thing
And there I saw a secret little door
And a bird began to sing:
"Happiness is just a tiny hole in a high and mighty wall
But me and you can easily go through if we can be small"

Pitiful and beautiful oh tiny little thing
I looked inside of me to see a tiny little thing
And there I lay, a baby in the hay
And a bird began to sing:
"Love is just a tiny hole in a high and mighty wall
But me and you can easily go through if we can be small"

Pitiful and beautiful oh tiny little thing
I climbed into a tree to see a tiny little thing
And there I spied a little bird had died
And a voice began to sing:
"Death is just a tiny hole in a high and mighty wall
But me and you can easily go through if we can be small".

Poem From Vasco Pyjama To Mr. Curly

My dearest Mister Curly
Today I woke up early
And made a little wish:
That we were flying fish,
Sparkling and free.
We jumped out of the sea
And flew up to the sun,
Then after that was done,
We went down to explore
The deepest ocean floor.
And so we did discover
The most amazing lover,
For what it may be worth,
It really is the earth.

Porn

If you're watching grubby porn;
Lonely, lustful and forlorn,
Feeling stupid, feeling low.
You'll feel better if you know
The energy that powers your screen
Is absolutely clean and green.

Prayer To Self

Gently swing from vine to vine,
Live from day to day,
Turning water into wine,
Loving what you may.

Learn to care and not to care,
Learn how not to know,
Feel your way from here to there,
Let it come and go.

Predator Drone

I was walking alone, when a predator drone
Started pointing its camera at me
And far, far away in the U.S. of A.
Sat a man with a Coke on his knee.

And he studied the scene that appeared on his screen
Of a strange little person alone
"What a dumb little jerk", he said with a smirk
And away flew the predator drone.

Profile

I work in a hell hole
I sleep in a tower
I drive through a tunnel
I dream in the shower
I cry in a gridlock
I fall on my face
I cringe in the mirror
I live in disgrace.

Radicalised

I was radicalised
by the butterflies
And later by a tree,
And then a word
from a passing bird
Put radical thoughts
in me.
And I am on the
watch-list now
With the fish and
the pixies too,
Who call to me
with a note of glee
"Just do what
you can do."

Real And Right And True *(Lullaby)*

Go your way now, all shall be well
Leave the day now, all shall be well
Go into the darkness, where the spark is
Real and right and true

Tiny birdie taught you to fly
Tiny baby taught you to cry
Out into the brightness where the light is
Real and right and true.

SAD *(Seasonal Affected Disorder)*

Spring, you great big wild erotic thing.
You activist. You revolution.
Nothing new but always new and sweet and shocking.

Insurgency of bees and snakes and flowers,
Of singing birds and ants and raging grass;
The crazy winds. The happy sun.
The mighty clouds of black in heaven.

Politicians, and celebrities, big mouths, big money,
You have no place in Spring except upon your knees.
Have respect; behold as life is born in freedom,
In truth, in thunder, in warmth, in danger.
In beauty and in joy.

In the wayward leap of bold cross-pollination.

Same Old

If we hear the same old dove
Singing in the same old tree
Might this bring us back to love
And beautiful simplicity?

But if we find no sign of these,
Instead, the same old politics,
The babbling celebrities,
A culture made from dirty tricks...

Could we see the same old cat
Sitting in the same old lane
And find some happy truth in that
And know of loveliness again?

Santa Santa

Santa, Santa in your sleigh,
Come and take my toys away
While I'm sleeping in my cot
Visit me and take the lot.

Santa, Santa set me free,
Clear an open space for me;
Me and all the girls and boys
Buried under heaps of toys.

Santa, Santa with your sack,
Come and take some plastic back;
Take it back and in its place,
Leave a little breathing space.

Scraps

Little scraps of peace and quiet,
Hope, conversation, handshakes –
All in dribs and drabs.
A few crumbs of fun,
A tiny flake of beauty,
One teaspoon of enthusiasm –
Offcuts of each other.
A skerrick of community,
A bit of a kiss.
A snippet of eye contact,
A snippet of hospitality,
A snippet of patience,
A shred of honour,
A wisp of good humour,
A sample of compassion –
Leftovers, oddments,
Remnants of the glorious situation.
A fragment of God,
Not much, really.
Sorry, time's up.

Sight

"Your sight is poor but your gaze is very gentle and friendly. How do you achieve this?"

"Well... I stare with love at lowly worms. I watch the silver stars at night...

I contemplate the coloured flowers. I gaze at dying butterflies..."

"Your sight is poor but your vision is beautiful."

Sitting On The Fence

Come sit down beside me
I said to myself,
And although it doesn't make sense
I held my own hand
As a small sign of trust
And together I sat on the fence.

Solitude

Solitude, a simple den,
A piece of paper and a pen,
A cup of tea, a piece of toast,
A window and the holy ghost.
Some calm, a table and a chair;
The mind is free, the soul is bare,
There's love to make and life to hold.
The ancient tiny thread of gold
That runs through all the joy and gloom
Is found inside this little room.

Something Nothing

He identified as a person with no identity:
A nobody, a nothing, a strange non-entity.
He wasn't quite the average bloke
He was beyond belief and beyond a joke;
Blank and hollow like an empty space
With a vacant smile upon his face
And a faraway look in his haunted eyes
Which made you think he might be wise;
An insightful genius with nothing dim.
In fact there were many who identified with him
And said he was cool and deep and amazing
But he said nothing and went on gazing;
Gazing at the sky, the floor, the wall,
Trying to think of nothing at all.

Spinebill

What a divine thrill
To see an Eastern Spinebill
Drinking from the flowers
In the sunny morning hours.

It hovers as it feeds
In delicate perfection
As three bright butterflies
Go whirling through the air
In the dance the heart can share
Pure love and joy in every direction.

In a world stuffed full
Of mad celebrities and ugly lies
Absurd, corrupted, vain and violent
This innocent sunlit morning surprise
So small and silent
Is the most holy moment you may ever find
Sometimes the morning can be kind.

Spring

Spring has come to Curly Flat
The swallow builds her nest of mud
And in her breast the pitter-pat
Of ancient music in her blood.

And in the tiny hearts of bees
The songs of many flowers are sung
As love entwines upon the breeze
With blossoms and the smell of dung.

The soil is ready, warm and willing
All the buds are bursting early
Empty hearts at last are filling
Life is good and sweet and curly.

Spring Baby

When Susan Crazy married Brian Mad
What a wild old time they had
During the reception;
Even a conception!

And nine months later little Loopy was born;
A home birth on the neighbour's lawn.
The whole street celebrated.
Her name was hyphenated.

Dear little Loopy Crazy-Mad
Had eyes like her mum and a
smile like her dad,
And just as we had feared;
Her mind was VERY weird.

Summer

Summer, oh you big hot thing
It's hard to know what you will bring.
Something golden? Something black?
You are such a maniac.

I planted three tomato plants,
I met a dog, we did a dance
Beneath the moon's old silver spell;
It makes tomatoes ripen well.

Or so I used to hear it said
By birds that landed on my head.
And so we dance to welcome back
The great amazing maniac.

Sweet Secret Peace

Real and right and true; the sky is blue;
Everlasting arms are holding you
Sweet secret peace
Sweet secret peace

Beautiful are you; your hands are new;
All you feel is real right and true
Sweet secret peace
Sweet secret peace

Real and right and true will turn into
The secret peace inside the heart of you
Sweet secret peace
Sweet secret peace
Sweet secret peace.

The Audacity Of Gloom

A bit of pessimism
Is a useful sort of prism
To keep beside your bed

It takes the morning light
And separates the bright
From all the dread

And then from out of dreamland
To gloomland and to gleamland
You have to go

How joyous, how depressing
That life is such a blessing
And such a blow.

The Cost

The cost of living's very high
The modern world will make you pay
Bits of you might have to die.
They'll make you give your soul away.

Feelings must be put on hold
Your spirit blocked, your peace is lost.
The heart becomes afraid and cold.
War is added to the cost.

This is what you pay for living,
Truth is mangled, beauty trashed,
The speed of life is unforgiving
Loving minds are mocked and bashed.

But there's an angel, she will love you
She is called sweet sanity
She is priceless, there above you,
She is there to make you free.

The Decline

Mental decline is a habit of mine
Bewilderment, dizziness, doubt
Again and again I can't get my brain
To grasp what this life is about.

You're no president and so you're not meant
To handle the data with ease
You wander alone as you search for your phone
Your glasses, your wallet, your keys.

But you know where to find those bits of your mind
That are friendly and peaceful and dumb
Don't knock it, don't spurn it you worked hard to earn it
This sweetness that you have become.

The Departed

Don't fret too much for the departed
Even though they leave you broken-hearted.
Have no fear,
They will reappear.

When you're alone and unprepared
They will just turn up. Do not be scared.
Be still. Do not turn away;
There is something wise they have come to say.

To you and to you alone;
Some plain and simple thing already known.
They will touch you and say,
'It's all right, everything will be okay.'

Or something just like that, short and clear,
Then casually they will turn and softly disappear,
Leaving you elated and in perfect peace;
The meaning of life and death will then increase.

And your love for the departed one will grow.
There is so much more you will get to know
About love that is unassailable
So long as you make yourself available.

The Factories Of War

I love the armament industry
The factories of war
It's good for the economy
That's what they do it for.
It's great for undertakers
For coffin makers too
For psychiatric nurses
There's lots of work to do.

The clergy will be busy
With many prayers and hymns
There'll be a boom in walking sticks
And artificial limbs.
The hospitals will be flat out
As surgeons make a pile
The head of state will celebrate
And wear that stupid smile.

The Gentle Hum

I wonder,
Will it all click into place?
I feel it might.
I had a glimpse
That things could all come right.
I'd wake up
On a sunny, slightly roostered morn
And wouldn't realise at first;
The rightness would take time to dawn.
And gradually
The thing would start to gleam;
This worried life I'd had,
This awful world, this painful mess –
It was, in fact, a kind of dream.
The penny would just drop
Into my hand,
The penny that I'd lost so long ago,
And all the peace withheld and blocked from me
Would start to flow.
The gentle hum, the gold and silver light
Would all resume;
The fairies and the pixies,
The particles of dust

Caught in the sunlight in my room.
I'd pick up
Where I'd been so rudely interrupted;
I'd have it back again for keeps,
My dog, my brilliant grasp of life,
My backyard and my paddocks full of time,
The world all glad around me,
My rightful place,
My joyous leaps.

The Glimmer

You have to wait for the gleam to start,
Patience will not hurt you
Glimmer seeks a weary heart,
Sadness is a virtue.

A cup of tea has been your prayer
And then without a warning,
A tiny sacred speck is there
Gleaming in the morning.

The simple glimmer has arrived,
Life has found a way
All that matters has survived
And love has saved the day.

The Handle

We give thanks for the invention of the handle.
Without it there would be many things we
couldn't hold on to.
As for the things we can't hold on to anyway,
let us gracefully accept their ungraspable nature
and celebrate all things elusive, fleeting and
intangible.
They mystify us and make us receptive to truth
and beauty. We celebrate and give thanks.

Amen.

The Heart Sings

The heart sings ⸴
A lullaby
To good natured things,
As there they lie;
Innocent and weary deep inside;
Worn out by the rushing tide
Of madness that has nearly drowned the day;
The clever malice that has had its way,
The bitterness and poison from above...
Rest your wings dear little dove.
The heart still sings to you of love.

The Little People

The little people have no say
Little people have no money
Little people have no way
To the land of milk and honey.

In a world of war and taxes
The little people must obey
Taking pills and having vaxes
Being careful what they say.

Little people, can they ever
Trust the slippery powers that be?
Stupidity has grown so clever
Madness can be had for free.

The Man Who Couldn't Cope

As I was hoping for some hope
I met a man who could not cope
"It's all too much" he said to me
"I do not like this world I see
The more I wander through the land
The less and less I understand.
The world is such a nasty mess.
And yet I also must confess
The sorrow and the shame it brings
To be a man who feels these things.
Oh how I wish that I could be
A joyful songbird in a tree."
And then I saw as off he went
The hope in disillusionment.

The Minister For Lovely Things

The Minister for lovely things
Writes poetry and paints and sings
And lives a humble simple life
Without a husband or a wife,
But with some angels in a tree
Where they enjoy philosophy
With birds or passing dogs or flowers,
Unconcerned by worldly powers.
This Minister for loveliness
Has got my vote I must confess.

The Missile

There is a missile, so I've heard
Which locks on to the smallest bird;
Finely tuned to seek and kill
A tiny chirp or gentle trill.

It's modern warfare's answer to
An ancient wisdom tried and true:
When fighting wars you first destroy
All songs of innocence and joy.

The Moment

Cometh the moment
Disappeareth the man
Could we please find him
Maybe you can
Honourable, decent
Moral and just
Steady compassionate
Worthy of trust
Courageous and loving
Capable, wise
Now is the moment
But where are the guys?

The Necessary Prince

He's a prince, he's been blessed,
He's on the spectrum, he's depressed,
He's got anxiety and addictions,
He has many strange afflictions,
He's not happy, he's not glorious,
He's been accused, he's notorious,
He's got worries, he's got scandals,
He burns both ends of many candles,
He is growing old and stale,
He's a patriarchal male,
He's pursued by paparazzi,
He gets called a creep, a Nazi,
Stupid, ugly, clumsy, dim,
We can all relate to him.
Though we groan and whine and wince
He's our necessary prince.

The Octopus

The octopus has many charms;
Eight fine legs - or are they arms?
And yet with such capacity
He stays within his territory.

Man with half as many limbs
But twice as many greedy whims
Breaks the boundaries everywhere
Creating sorrow and despair.

And with brutality or stealth
He seizes other people's wealth,
Their land, their art, their sacred bliss;
The octopus does not do this!

The Other You

... and who is that happy soul beside you,
so unabashed holding that great big bunch of flowers;

... holding your arm and singing that trashy song you love
in secret;

... the trashy song that brings you to a halt; brings you to
your knees; brings you to your precious tears of happiness?

Who is that?

Who is that tickling the palm of your hand and whispering
in your ear "Yes! Go on; I dare you"

Who is it that clears your mess while you sleep;
Who waits calmly for your awakening;
Who loves you from afar?

Could it be?
Could it possibly be?
Yes, it is.
Of course it is. It's...
THE OTHER YOU!

The Path To Your Door

The path to your door
Is the path within,
Is made by animals,
Is lined by thorns,
Is stained with wine,
Is lit by the lamp of sorrowful dreams,
Is washed with joy,
Is swept by grief,
Is blessed by the lonely traffic of art,
Is known by heart,
Is known by prayer,
Is lost and found,
Is always strange,
The path to your door.

The Plot

'He's lost the plot,' they say,
But it simply isn't true;
You cannot lose the plot,
It's stuck to you!

Nor can it be chucked out
Or thrown into a pit;
You can't just dump the plot,
You're stuck to it!

But you can soak the plot
And loosen it with tears
And slowly peel it back.
It could take years.

And you can lose your face
And you can lose a lot
And feel blessed when they say,
'He's lost the plot!'

The Room

Sick of reading the room?
Go outside and read the garden.
Read the birds and the moon.
Read the tea leaves in your cup.
Read the stars, feel the clouds.
Read the palm of your hand.
Read the eyes of a child.
Watch the ants as they work.
Touch the truth in the soil.
Listen to the thunder and the rain.
Read a poem.
Stay away from the room.
Reading the room is a waste of life.
It will make you sick!

The Smile

I shot a smile into the air
It fell to earth I know not where
Perhaps on someone else's face
In some forgotten, quiet place.

Perhaps somewhere a sleeping child
Has had a happy dream and smiled
Or some old soul about to die
Has smiled and made a little sigh.

Has sighed a simple final prayer
That lifts up gently in the air
And flows into the world so wild,
Perhaps to wake the sleeping child.

The Stink

Terrible sleazebags made into lords
Horrible creeps winning noble awards
Everyday people trudge through the dirt
Shaking their heads as they swallow the hurt.

Leaders and liars grin from on high
Flaunting their medals and carving the pie
Parading their greed but unable to hide
The stink in the land when honour has died.

The scum always floats to the top, it is said
It's as old as the hills and as cold as the dead
It stinks to high heaven, it's darker than crime.
The slippery slope and the slippery slime.

The Symptoms

The death we meet is never late
And never early.
The way ahead is never straight,
It's always curly.

Loveliness is crystal clear
And yet it's pearly,
Far away is very near,
And always curly.

The Value Of The Soul

The value of the soul plunged yesterday to its lowest level in five years.

One person invested in a smile.

A meteor plummeted and a few wishes were made.

Experts said nothing.

There were rumours about a small child who had flown over the city on a carpet of rose petals.

Certain things slid and crashed but a cheer rose up and a dog barked playfully. A violin was heard too.

The Wagon Of Hope

The wagon of hope
Is pulled by ducks
Two fine ducks
As white as snow

The boat of faith
Is kept afloat
By stars above
And fish below

The way ahead
Is known to birds
Is told by birds
Each day at dawn

While the song of doom
Composed by men
Is played upon
A paper horn.

The Wall

"Love in spite of all" it said.
In delicate letters wild and small.
And like a man raised from the dead
He saw the writing on the wall.

Upon this wall that blocked his life
Was scratched a message brief and bare
By an angel with a pocket knife
And genius enough to care.

As grim as any wall could be
A wall of cruelty, shame and dread
It bore the words to set him free
"Love in spite of all" it said.

The Wee Dark Hours

The angel of the wee dark hours
Visits you and brings you flowers
And lays them on your worried heart
And turns your darkness into art;
A leap of faith, an act of love,
A vision from the stars above
And all your troubles on this earth
Can find redemption and rebirth
In fragrance from these happy flowers
That lead you through the wee dark hours.

The World That Lives

The world I live in is at war
With the world that lives in me.
I shelter in a child's heart
And in a dream I see,
Beauty, joy and innocence,
An angel in a tree.

May I die here with this love
And feel this heart go free,
And bless this world in which I live
That gave my world to me.

Things Just Seem To Fall Apart

Things just seem to fall apart,
String bags full of oranges
And things within the heart;

Calamities evaporate and memories depart.
People laugh at anything
And things just fall apart.

This Day

This day before you now
Greet her with love and joy.
She is a fine strong person:
This precious living day
She is young and old
She is warm and cold
She is here for you
She will hold you well.
Make love with her
You'd be a fool to turn away
She is here. She is yours.
She is wise, she is hers.
She has dawned on you; this epic day.
Do not underestimate what she can do
Give thanks for her as you make your way.
Give thanks for the power and the kindness
Of this precious living day.

Tiny Little Boat

God bless this tiny little boat
And me who travels in it;
It stays afloat for years and years
And sinks within a minute.
And so the soul in which we sail
Unknown by years of thinking
Is deeply felt and understood
The minute that it's sinking.

To Spring

Thank God. At last! Spring is coming.
I can hear the bees inside me humming.
The mind becomes a flower bed.
A nest is being built upon my head.
The spirit rises from its tomb.
The weary soul is coming into bloom.
We've made it through. We will survive.
The soil is sweet and love is still alive.
The bell of happiness is ringing.
A little bird inside your heart is singing.

To Sybil

We do it for the common good:
Obedience and submission.
We crawl as we are told we should
Against our intuition.
Except for Sybil, what a girl,
She'll set your heart astir;
Sybil Disobedience,
We'd love some time with her.

Traffic Nurse

So as the traffic jams get worse
It might be wise to have a nurse
Inside the vehicle with you;
A therapist to help you through
The moments when it's highly strung;
The waggy tail, the pinkish tongue,
The happy gaze, the panting breath
Will soothe away the fear of death.

Twinkle Twinkle Little Star

Twinkle, twinkle little star
What a boring thing you are
When compared to fireworks
Stars are lonely, loser jerks.
Twinkle twinkle little star
How embarrassing you are.

Underpants Which Have In Winter Sagged (a hymn for Spring)

Underpants which have, in winter sagged
And fallen into darkness and despond
Shall from their shame and loneliness be dragged
And laid upon the fern's emerging frond.
The frond shall gently rise to greet the spring,
Above the flowers, into the sun fantastic,
Where birds in praise of underpants shall sing
And life will be restored to old elastic.

Undiagnosed

The thing I love the most
Is to be undiagnosed
I want to be a mystery to myself
Unexplained and inconclusive
Unto myself elusive
Like a spirit or a pixie or an elf.

And this moonlit part of me
So untroubled and so free
Would never understand but could adore.
As I'd wander and I'd beam
With a deep unknowing gleam
And I'd see a world I'd never seen before.

Unwell

All the world's great work
is done
Without ambition to excel
By people who proceed
unsung
And feel a little bit
unwell.

Up And Down

I used to watch the sun go down
But now I watch the world go down
I sit and watch the world go down
It hurts to watch the world go down.

I used to see the sun come up
And still I see the sun come up
I wake and watch the sun come up
It's good to see the sun come up.

Vasco Pyjama's New Poem For Mr. Curly

When man came down
out of the trees
In pre-historic times
And learned to hate
and calculate
And cultivate his crimes
The trees continued
growing strong
Their branches full
of yearning
Each graceful limb
a sacred hymn
To sing of man's returning.

Viral

Every man's a virus
Every woman too
Everyone's infectious
This is what we do
We spread the love around
We spread the hate as well
We give each other heaven
We give each other hell.
We catch it from each other
We get it from the moon
Everyone's contagious
No one is immune.

Vote

Little tiny precious vote,
Underneath my overcoat,
Snug and warm against my heart,
You and I will have to part.

I must cast you to the horde,
With your little wooden sword,
And your hopeful marching song;
Little vote of mine be strong.

Should our happy cause be dashed,
And your wooden sword be smashed,
Come back, dear beloved vote,
Dream inside my overcoat.

Well Connected Goat

I saw a goat one frosty morn
With the moon upon his horn,
With a star upon his tail,
With a bird upon his back,
With a flower upon his nose,
With his feet upon a rock,
With his eyes upon the ground,
With the frost upon his coat.
Good morning, well connected goat!

When Love Has Been Neglected

When love has been neglected
It can only be expected
That in the space love used to fill
A nasty terror cell then will
Take form and soon take hold;
A fearful little mould.

So if you have the wish
Take your Petri dish
And cultivate a cell of love
And by the moon and stars above,
In reverence and in duty,
Nourish it with beauty.

When The Heart

When the heart
Is cut or cracked or broken,
Do not clutch it;
Let the wound lie open.

Let the wind
From the good old sea blow in
To bathe the wound with salt,
And let it sting.

Let a stray dog lick it,
Let a bird lean in the hole and sing
A simple song like a tiny bell,
And let it ring.

Win And Beat
(a song with a jaunty tune)

Win and beat, win and beat
Everybody must compete
Life can never be complete
Unless you win and beat.

Win the prize, win the prize
Beat the others down to size
Love it as they agonise
When you win the prize.

Win the trophy, win the award.
With the pen and with the sword
With integrity and fraud
Win the great award.

Win the war, win the war
That's what life on earth is for
You'll be rich and they'll be poor
When you win the war.

Winter

A storm in a tea cup;
A thundery thing,
The rain tumbles down and
the heart starts to sing.
A flicker of lightning,
the sky starts to drop,
The flowers in the vase
do a strange little hop.
The candle flame wobbles,
A tiny bell rings,
My cup runneth over with
beautiful things.

Winter Prayer

The little frog in joyful praise has croaked
The winter's quiet heavenly fog has come.
The paddocks and the bush are softly cloaked
In peaceful beautiful delirium.

Oh holy mist come to our heart and mind
Come gently to the troubles and the pains
Make soft the angry shapes that clash and grind
Make beautiful the scars and ugly stains.

Yet listen for the joyful frog, and thrill.
Look softly as the mist of love comes in.
Be still, forgive, adore with all your will,
And touch the softer, simpler world within.

Winter's Come

Winter's come and I am glum
And that's a lovely thing.
It sweeps away the sheer dismay
That human beings bring.

Winter please, just make me freeze
And cool my burning brain:
My overheated, much repeated
Existential pain.

Make me feel intensely real
And lash me as you choose
So I won't dwell, upon the hell
Of people in the news.

Wish List

Sanity, beauty, kindness, care
All so simple if you dare
Sweet forgiveness, patience, peace,
Chickens, blackbirds, ducks and geese.
Trees and flowers, grass and seeds,
Hands and feet and coloured beads.
Cups of tea and distant bells
Clouds and mountains, cooking smells,
A garden path, a wooden chair,
Sanity, beauty, kindness, care.

Writer

Is there in this life a nook
Not described in some damned book;
Or in the heart a little bird
Not yet captured by a word;
Or in the soul a tiny breath
Which hasn't been described to death —
Something lovelier and lighter
Than the craft of some damned writer?